Cecilia McDowall

A Time for all Seasons
Before Words Fail

for soprano solo, upper voices, SSATB, piano, and optional percussion

MUSIC DEPARTMENT

OXFORD
UNIVERSITY PRESS

OXFORD
UNIVERSITY PRESS

Great Clarendon Street, Oxford, OX2 6DP,
United Kingdom

Oxford University Press is a department of the University of Oxford.
It furthers the University's objective of excellence in research, scholarship,
and education by publishing worldwide. Oxford is a registered trade mark of
Oxford University Press in the UK and in certain other countries

First published in 2016

Impression: 2

ISBN 978-0-19-341148-7

Printed in Great Britain on acid-free paper by
Halstan & Co. Ltd, Amersham, Bucks

Composer's note

At the heart of *A Time for all Seasons* lies the extraordinary text from Ecclesiastes 3: 1–8—'To every thing there is a season'. The poetry of these universal and familiar words has been set in context by the award-winning author and poet Kevin Crossley-Holland, who, by reworking these verses, has brought a present-day perspective to the cantata in a subtle and evocative fashion.

The upper (or children's) voices thread a running commentary in both the first and last sections; at the start they sing an abbreviated first line of the Ecclesiastes text, and in the last—'There is nothing new under the sun'—present a prescient reminder of how things are and will be. The choir begins the work in a joyous mood, but then moves on to a more contemplative appraisal of reality. The soprano solo brings a relaxed and slightly jazzy flavour to the words 'When sudden birdsong is alarming', but is cut off by the return of the opening choral material.

In the bright middle section the upper voices sing the words of Ecclesiastes—'a time to plant, and a time to pluck up that which is planted'—with interjections from the sopranos and altos of the main choir. The soprano solo leads into the final section which, in the face of possible catastrophe, urges us to draw 'near to your creator'. Underlying the closing part of the work is a phrase taken from the 13th-century Latin sequence *Dies irae*—a musical premonition, perhaps, of things to come. The upper voices have the last word.

The work was originally conceived for soprano solo, children's choir, community choir, SSATB chorus, piano, and optional percussion. Here, the children's choir and community choir parts have been combined into a single part for upper voices, which could be performed equally well by an upper-voice, children's, or community choir.

Separate parts for upper-voice choir and percussion are available to download from www.oup.com.

A Time for all Seasons was commissioned by Harlow Chorus for its 40th anniversary. It was first performed in April 2016 by Emily Yarrow (soprano), Susan Graham Smith (piano), Graham Instrall (percussion), Harlow Chorus, Harlow Chorus Training Choir, and Harlow Children's Choir, conducted by Alexander Chaplin.

Duration: *c.*18 minutes

Text

A Time for all Seasons
Before Words Fail

*To every thing there is a season, and a time to every
purpose under the heaven:
A time to be born, and a time to die;*

Before shoulders sag and stick-legs buckle,
before teeth rattle and eyes grow misty

Before heights become fearsome and
journeys troublesome

When sudden birdsong is alarming, and
sweet daughters sing out of tune

When even honey bees are irksome though
the apple is in blossom

Before desire slackens

Before the alphabet scrambles, before
words fail:

*a time to plant, and a time to pluck up that which
is planted;
A time to kill, and a time to heal; a time to break
down, and a time to build up;
A time to weep, and a time to laugh; a time to
mourn, and a time to dance;
A time to cast away stones, and a time to gather
stones together; a time to embrace, and a time to
refrain from embracing;
A time to get, and a time to lose; a time to keep,
and a time to cast away;
A time to rend, and a time to sew; a time to keep
silence, and a time to speak;
A time to love, and a time to hate; a time of war,
and a time of peace.*

The wind drives south, the wind
wafts north...
One generation stumbles, the next skips
and dances in...
There is nothing new under the sun

Before deadly clouds mass and close ranks

Before grids seize and turbines fall silent,
before the sea curdles

Before plates grind and widen and this poor
planet spins

Before the hub blackens and explodes,
before the moon wastes and constellations
are snuffed out

Before dust falls to dust and the spirit soars:
with a handful of quietness draw near to
your creator.

Ecclesiastes 3: 1–8 (King James Version)
Kevin Crossley-Holland (b. 1941)

Commissioned by Harlow Chorus in their 40th anniversary season

A Time for all Seasons

Before Words Fail

Kevin Crossley-Holland (b. 1941)
Ecclesiastes 3, vv. 1–8

CECILIA McDOWALL

*Optional Percussion: Suspended Cymbal, Tambourine, Triangle

Music © Oxford University Press 2016. Text © Kevin Crossley-Holland 2016.

Printed in Great Britain

OXFORD UNIVERSITY PRESS, MUSIC DEPARTMENT, GREAT CLARENDON STREET, OXFORD OX2 6DP

and a time to die, there is a sea - son.

and a time to die, there is a sea - son.

and a time to die, there is a sea - son.

and a time to die, there is a sea - son.

Be -

Be -

*This part may alternatively be sung by a children's choir

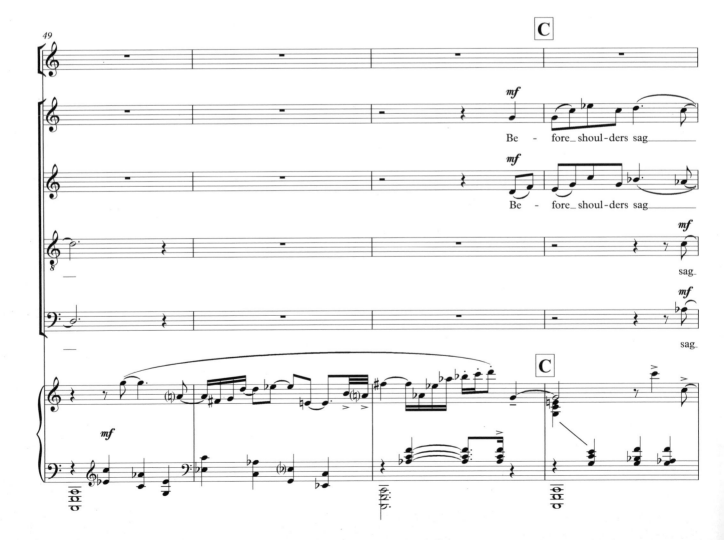

tune, When e-ven ho-ney bees are

irk - some though the ap-ple is in blos-som, is in blos - som,_____ ah_____

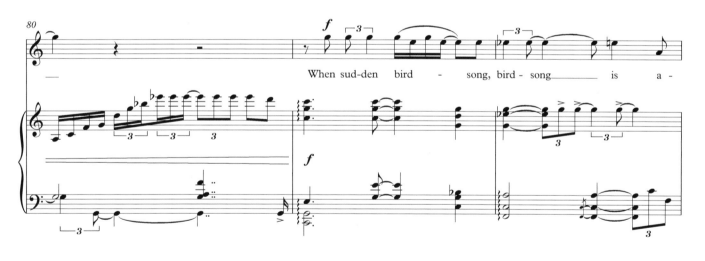

_____ When sud-den bird - song, bird - song_____ is a-

-larm - ing_____ and_ sweet daugh-ters sing, sing_____ out of tune, sing out of

(con Ped.)

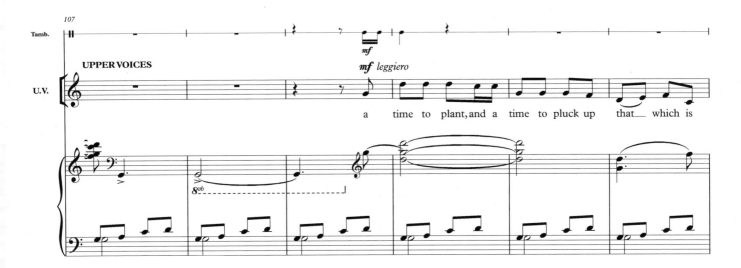

Tamb.

UPPER VOICES

U.V.

mf leggiero

a time to plant, and a time to pluck up that which is

plant - ed;_____ A time to kill, and a time to____ heal, a time____ to____

heal;_____ A time to kill and a time to heal; a

time____ to____ break down,_____ and a time to build, to

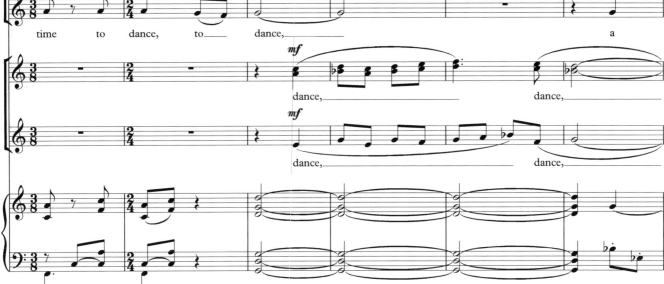

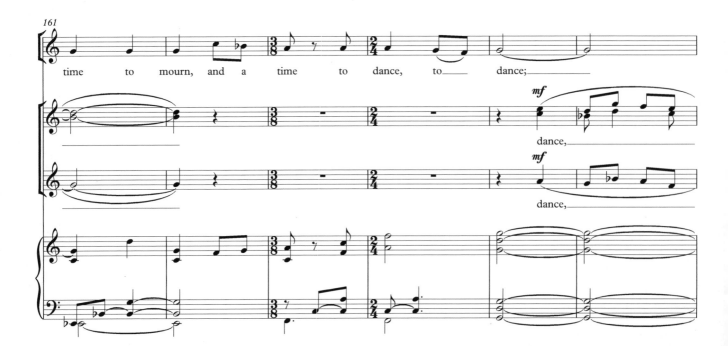

185

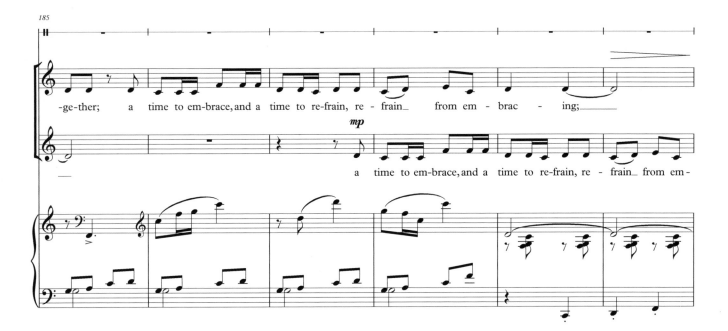

-ge-ther; a time to em-brace, and a time to re-frain, re - frain_ from em - brac - ing;_

_ a time to em-brace, and a time to re-frain, re - frain_ from em-

191

-brac - ing;_

197

a time to keep, and a time to cast a-

A time to get, and a time to lose; a time to keep, and a time to cast a-

UPPER VOICES 1 & 2

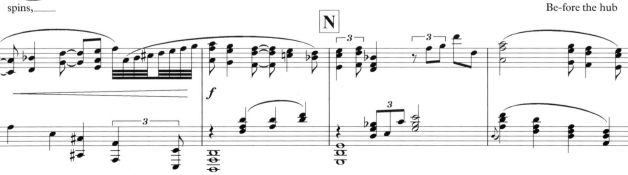

*Dies irae sequence

339

S. Solo: to____ your cre-a____-tor.____

U.V.: there is no-thing new,____

S.: dust,____ dust,____

A.: dust,____ dust,____

T.: dust,____ dust,____

B.: dust,____ dust,____

343 Triangle

Tri.

U.V.: there is no-thing new,____ there is no-thing new.____

S.: dust,____ dust.____

A.: dust,____ dust.____

T.: dust,____ dust.____

B.: dust,____ dust.____

ritardando   lunga